British Cars of the 1960s

1969 Rover P6 2000

Montpelier Publishing

ISBN: 9798862872620

Published in Great Britain by Montpelier Publishing.

Printed and distributed by Amazon.

Introduction

The 1960s were a transformative period for British car manufacturing, marked by innovation, cultural shifts, and economic challenges. Despite the Second World War's economic aftermath, and heightened competition from global automakers, this era witnessed the creation of iconic vehicles that would shape automotive history.

Innovations like the Mini Cooper, designed by Sir Alec Issigonis and produced by the British Motor Corporation (BMC), became symbols of the decade. The Mini's compact size, affordability, and rally successes, particularly in the Monte Carlo Rally, earned it legendary status.

The E-Type Jaguar, unveiled in 1961, blended striking design with exhilarating performance, epitomizing British automotive excellence and glamour.

Furthermore, industry consolidation resulted in the formation of the British Leyland Motor Corporation (BLMC) in 1968, despite facing various challenges.

The 1960s also linked car design with pop culture, as British cars became emblems of rebellion and self-expression. This era celebrated visionaries, engineers, and workers who defined a golden age of British car manufacturing.

Alvis TE21

1963-1966

2993 cc engine

130 bhp

107 mph top speed

Power steering

Credit: Steve Glover

Alvis TF21

1966-1967

Last Alvis to be built

2993 cc engine

150 bhp

120 mph top speed

Credit: Rick Johnson

Aston Martin DB5

Credit: DeFacto

1963-1965

3995cc I6 engine

282-325 bhp

Aluminium engine

145mph top speed

Aston Martin DB6

Credit: Brian Snelson

1965-1970

3995cc I6 engine

282 bhp

Split bumpers

AC option

Austin 1100/1300

1963-1974

Hydrolast suspension

Morris, Riley, Wolseley and MG versions

Best selling British car of 1960s

Credit: Charles01r

Austin 3 Litre

1967-1971

2912cc engine

Hydrolast suspension

125 bhp

Wood veneer interior

Credit: Calreyn88

Austin 1800/2200 'Landcrab'

Credit: DeFacto

1964-1975

Morris and Wolseley versions

Dashboard handbrake

Front split bench seat

Hydrolast suspension

Austin Maxi

Credit: John Shepherd

1969-1981

First British hatchback

Front wheel drive

5-speed gearbox

1485cc engine

90mph top speed

Bentley T1

1965-1977

6230 cc V8 engine

Unibody

118 mph top speed

Independent suspension

Credit: Anchor Network

Bond 875

1965-1970

Three wheeler

875 cc engine

34 bhp

882lb kerb weight

Credit: Charles01

Bond Equipe

1963-1970

1147cc I6 engine

63-75 bhp

Fibreglass body

Triumph Herald chassis

Bristol 4 series

1961-1969

5211cc V8 Chrysler engine

Power steering

Push-button transmission

250 hp

Daimler 250

1962-1969

2.5 L engine

Jaguar body

112 mph top speed

19 mpg

Cost £1647 (1962)

Credit: Riley

Daimler Majestic Major

1960-1968

Twin exhausts

4561cc V8 engine

120 mph top speed

Power disc brakes

Credit: Chris Sampson

Daimler DS240 Limousine

Credit: Alexandre Prevot

1968-1992

4235cc I6 engine

226" length

Interior partition

6 passenger seats

Daimler Sovereign

Credit: John Lloyd

1961-1969

2.5L V8 engine

V12 engine version

Four headlights

Sister car to Jaguar 420

Ford Capri Mk1

1969-1974

1.3 to 5 litre engines

Live rear axle

1.9 million sold

Collapsible steering column

Credit: Order 242

Ford Consul Classic

1961-1963

Syncromesh gears

1340 cc

'Greased for life' bearings

Column or floor mounted gear change

Credit: Allen Watkin

Ford Anglia Super 123E

1962-1967

1198cc engine

Two-tone paint option

41.2mpg

Kerb weight 1642lb

Ford Corsair

1963-1970

1498 to 1996 cc engine

Aerodynamic bodywork

Reversing lights

Top speed 110 mph

Ford Cortina Mk1

1962-1966

1200 or 1500 cc engine

Synchromesh transmission

Front disc brakes

'Aeroflow' ventilation

Ford Cortina Mk2

1966-1970

1200 to 1600 cc engines

'Rostyle' wheels

Lotus rally version

Self-adjusting brakes

Ford Escort Mk1

Credit: Tim Green

1967-1975

Rack-and-pinion steering

1100/1300cc engine

40-63 hp

McPherson struts

Gordon-Keeble

Credit: Alan Watkin

1964-1967

5.4L V8 Chevrolet engine

300 hp

Glass fibre body

Twin petrol tanks

Hillman Imp

1963-1976

Diaphragm spring clutch

Auto choke

875cc rear engine

Cost £508 (1963)

Credit: Charles01

Hillman Super Minx

1961-1967

1592cc engine

62 bhp

80 mph top speed

Also badged as Singer Vogue

Credit: Brian Snelson

Humber Sceptre Mk1

Credit: Tim Green

1963-1965

Based on Hillman Minx

1592cc engine

95.8mph top speed

0-60 in 12.5 seconds

Jaguar 420

Credit: Mr Choppers

1966-1969

4.2 litre inline 6 engine

Variable power steering

245 bhp

16 mpg

Jaguar E Type

1961-1974

3.8/4.2L
engine

0-60 in 6.4
seconds

150 mph top
speed

Up to 283 lb/ft
torque

Credit: DeFacto

Jaguar Mark X (420G)

1961-1970

Torsion
sprung doors

3.8 or 4.2 L
engine

Top speed
120 mph

Unibody

Credit: Jiri Sedlacek

Jaguar S Type

1963-1968

3.4/3.8L engine

Disc brakes

Overdrive option

Independent rear suspension

Jaguar XJ1

1968-1973

2.8 or 4.2 litre engine

Twin fuel tanks

Optional AC

Borg-Warner transmission

Jensen CV8

1962-1966

5.9 or 6.3 litre
V8 engine

Fibreglass
body

136 mph top
speed

0-60 in 6.7
seconds

Credit: Charles01

Jensen FF

1966-1971

Four wheel
drive

ABS braking

6.3L V8
engine

Torqueflite
auto
transmission

Credit: Calreyn88

Jensen Interceptor

Credit: Phil

1966-1976

6.3 litre engine

270 hp

Steel body

Rear wheel drive with limited slip differential

Land Rover Series IIA

Credit: Cahrles01

1961-1971

2.25 L petrol or diesel engine

Front bench seat

Servo assisted brakes

Lotus Elan

1962-1973

1558 cc
engine

4 disc brakes

Fibreglass
body

Steel
backbone
chassis

Credit:Sicnag

Lotus Europa

1966-1975

Fibreglass
body

1470 cc rear
engine

82 hp at
6000 rpm

Removable
side windows

Credit: Draco2008

MG MGB

Credit:Andrew Bone

1963-1968

1798cc I6
engine

0-60 in 11
seconds

Unibody

95 hp
at 5400 rpm

MG Midget

Credit: Oxyman

1961-1979

948cc engine

56hp at 5500
rpm

87.9 mph
top speed

0-60 in 18.3
seconds

Morris Minor 1000 Series V

1962-1971

1098 cc
engine

Unibody

77 mph top
speed

Baulk-ring
synchromesh
transmission

Credit: Tim Green

Mini Clubman

1969-1980

Disc brakes

998 or 1275
cc engine

38 bhp

90 mph top
speed

Disc brakes

Credit: DeFacto

Mini Cooper (S)

Credit: Andrew Bone

1961-1971

998/1071cc race-tuned engine

Twin tanks

Disc brakes

Close-ratio gearbox

Mini Traveller/Countryman

Credit: Bristol404

1960-1969

84 inch chassis

Austin/Morris badging

Front and rear folding seats

Wood trim

Peel P50

1962-1965

49cc engine

World's smallest production car

38 mph top speed

54" long by 39" wide

Credit: Andrew Bone

Peel Trident

1965-1966

Three wheeler

49 or 99 cc engine

Two-seater

100 mpg

Price £190

Credit: Charles01

Reliant Regal 3/25

Credit: Chris Samson

1962-1968

600cc aluminium engine

Three-wheeler

Fibreglass body

25 bhp

Reliant Rebel

1964-1974

600 or 700 cc engine

Kerb weight 1185lb

Four wheel version of Reliant Regal

65 mpg

Reliant Sabre

1961-1963

1703 cc Ford Consul engine

Fibreglass body

90 mph top speed

73 bhp

Credit: Alan Walker

Reliant Scimitar GT SE4

1964-1970

2.6 litre Ford Zodiac engine

117 mph top speed

120 bhp

Cost £1292

Credit: Calreyn 88

Riley Elf/Wolseley Hornet

Credit :DeFacto

1961-1969

Upmarket version of Mini

34 bhp

848 cc engine

Leather seats

Wooden dash

Rolls Royce Silver Shadow

Credit: Ermell

1965-1976

6230cc or 6750 cc V8 engine

Self levelling suspension

Automatic transmission

172/189 hp

Rootes Arrow (Hillman Hunter)

1966-1979

1496 or 1725 cc engine

66/89 hp

Power assisted brakes

Driver's side handbrake

Credit: Charles01

Rover P5 MkII/III

1962-1973

3 or 3.5 litre aluminium engine

Top speed 95 mph

115 bhp

20.5 mpg

Credit: Oxyman

Rover P6 (Rover 2000)

Credit: Anidat

1963-1977

2, 2.2 or 3 litre engine

Full synchromesh

Unibody

Dunlop 'run flat' tyres

Singer Gazelle VI

Credit: Alan Watkin

1965-1967

1725 cc engine

Five bearing crankshaft

Optional overdrive

59 bhp

Sunbeam Tiger

1964-1967

4.3 litre Ford V8 engine

Unibody

120 mph top speed

4-speed synchromesh gearbox

Credit: Steve Brown

Sunbeam Alpine Series II-V

1965-1970

31 mpg

1592 or 1725cc engine

Front disc brakes

99.5 mph top speed

Credit: Robert G

Sunbeam Rapier H120

Credit: Andrew Bone

1968-1976

1725cc I6 engine

Rostyle wheels

Rear spoiler

106 mph top speed

Triumph 1300

Credit: Kitmaster

1965-1970

1296cc engine

Adjustable steering wheel

Wooden dashboard

61 hp

Triumph 2000

1963-1977

2 or 2.5 litre engine

90 bhp

Overdrive option

Fuel injection

Credit: Anchor Network

Triumph Spitfire

1962-1980

1147 or 1296 cc engine

Triumph Herald chassis

Bolt-on winter hard top option

Credit: Avaldia

Triumph Herald 1200

Credit: Ch...

1961-1970

1147cc engine

39 bhp

Disc brake option

Estate and coupe versions

Triumph TR4

Credit: Jeremy

1961-1967

2088cc I4 engine

Independent rear suspension

Body design by Michelotti

71 hp

Triumph Vitesse

1962-1971

1596 or 1998 cc engine

Sunroof option

Wooden dashboard

Top speed 91 mph

Credit: Simon Speed

Vanden Plas Princess R

1964-1968

4 litre Rolls-Royce engine

175 bhp

Top speed 112 mph

Rear seat tables

Credit: Red Simon

Vauxhall Viva HA

Credit:Vauxford

1963-1966

1057cc engine

44 bhp

Based on Opel Kadett

4 speed synchromesh gearbox

Vauxhall Viva HB

Credit: Bristol404

1966-1970

1159 or 1599cc engine

Twin-carb 1975 GT version

12 gallon fuel tank

Wolseley 16/60

1961-1971

1489 cc engine

Illuminated grill badge

76.6 mph top speed

Hydraulic braking

Credit: Allen Watkin

Wolseley 6/110

1961-1968

Overdrive option

2.9 litre engine

Borg Warner auto transmission option

Credit: Red Simon

Other large print books from Montpelier Publishing:

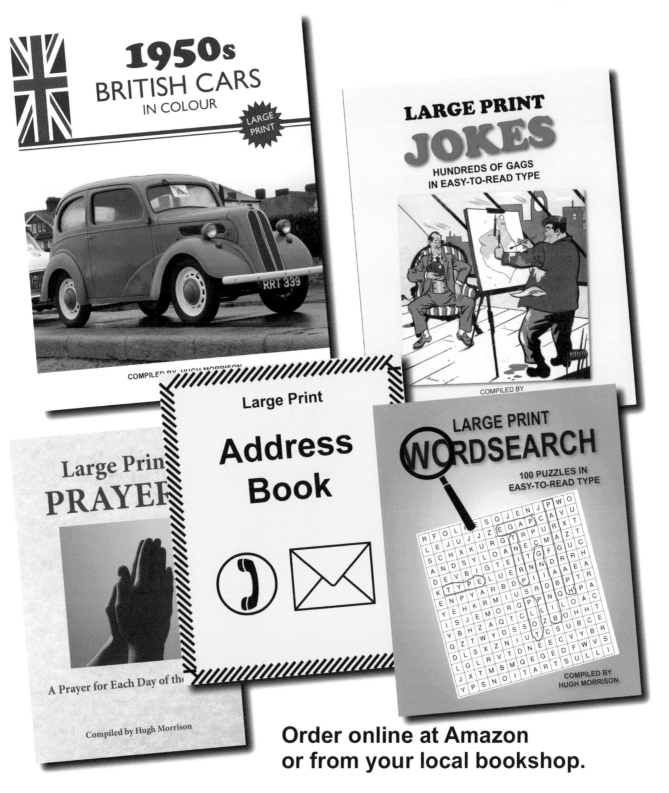

1950s BRITISH CARS IN COLOUR

LARGE PRINT

LARGE PRINT JOKES
HUNDREDS OF GAGS IN EASY-TO-READ TYPE

COMPILED BY

Large Print PRAYER

A Prayer for Each Day of the

Compiled by Hugh Morrison

Large Print
Address Book

LARGE PRINT WORDSEARCH
100 PUZZLES IN EASY-TO-READ TYPE

COMPILED BY HUGH MORRISON

Order online at Amazon or from your local bookshop.

Printed in Great Britain
by Amazon

47294884R00023